A Meditation Journey for Beginners

Cheryl Forrest

BALBOA.
PRESS
A DIVISION OF HAY HOUSE

Balboa Press books may be ordered through booksellers or by contacting:

Balboa Press
A Division of Hay House
1663 Liberty Drive
Bloomington, IN 47403
www.balboapress.com
1 (877) 407-4847

Because of the dynamic nature of the Internet, any web addresses or links contained in this book may have changed since publication and may no longer be valid. The views expressed in this work are solely those of the author and do not necessarily reflect the views of the publisher, and the publisher hereby disclaims any responsibility for them.

The author of this book does not dispense medical advice or prescribe the use of any technique as a form of treatment for physical, emotional, or medical problems without the advice of a physician, either directly or indirectly. The intent of the author is only to offer information of a general nature to help you in your quest for emotional and spiritual well-being. In the event you use any of the information in this book for yourself, which is your constitutional right, the author and the publisher assume no responsibility for your actions.

Any people depicted in stock imagery provided by Thinkstock are models, and such images are being used for illustrative purposes only. Certain stock imagery © Thinkstock.

Print information available on the last page.

ISBN: 978-1-5043-4321-3 (sc)
ISBN: 978-1-5043-4322-0 (hc)
ISBN: 978-1-5043-4323-7 (e)

Library of Congress Control Number: 2015916811

Balboa Press rev. date: 11/30/2015

I dedicate this book to all my students. You are each my greatest mentor and my greatest source of inspiration.

Acknowledgments

Thank you to my husband, who I cannot do anything without. And thank you to my dear friend Midge for your help and insight and great sense of humor. This book would not have come together without you both.

Contents

Welcome to Meditation

Some form of meditation has been practiced as a spiritual discipline within all of our religions for thousands of years. Humanity has used numerous techniques over the centuries to heal, communicate with nature, contact "the gods," and explore our inner landscapes.

The practice of meditation stayed strong and spread widely through the East. Only recently has the West taken interest in the practice of meditation. The '60s with their use of drugs opened up an inner world that intrigued, surprised, and frightened us. The '70s brought about a consciousness revolution. Transcendental meditation (TM) began the process of legitimizing meditation—specifically to reduce stress and stress-related illnesses. Biofeedback and an interest in altered states of consciousness, as well as research into the specialized functions of the brain hemispheres, led us forward and inward.

Today we have a growing body of scientific research showing that simply turning inward helps numerous health issues and even changes brain function. It is now embraced by people all across the globe. Its practice has proved that ten to fifteen minutes of meditation a day can keep us mentally and physically in peak condition. More importantly, it seems to lead us to a greater personal sense of fulfilment and contentment.

Meditation has definitely become a part of our culture. On any given day you will find articles about new research and the benefits of meditation in newspapers, fitness magazines, health magazines, scientific and medical journals, spiritual books and magazines, and Google and on YouTube. It is showing up in movies, documentaries, talk shows, and sitcoms.

And now, more importantly it is about to become a part of your journey.

Someone e-mailed the following list to me. I often hand it out in my classes or counseling sessions.

Reasons to Meditate

+ Increase your libido
+ Reduce PMS
+ Pain relief
+ Reach your ideal weight
+ Allow you to sleep less (or more)
+ Reduce your blood pressure
+ Reduce chronic diseases
+ Aid digestion
+ Slow aging
+ Overcome addiction
+ Heal headaches and migraines
+ Improve motor performance skills
+ Lessen the activity of viruses
+ Reduce arthritis pain
+ Strengthen your immune system
+ Eliminate insomnia
+ Reduce hypertension
+ Increase endocrine system function
+ Restore your body's natural pH balance
+ Help in post-operative healing
+ Boost serotonin levels
+ Increase growth hormone
+ Increase longevity
+ Relax your nervous system
+ Decrease muscle tension
+ Increase physical relaxation
+ Increase your body's level of DHEA
+ Waste less energy
+ Boost melatonin
+ Decrease respiratory rate
+ Gives you whole brain synchronization
+ Lower oxygen consumption
+ Increase circulation and slow heart rate
+ Decrease cortisol levels
+ Helps with infertility
+ Reduce the need for medical care
+ Boost endorphins
+ Lower cholesterol
+ Breathe easier
+ Relief from asthma
+ Become more emotionally stable
+ Reduce anxiety

- Help with PTSD
- Improve relationships
- Reduce depression
- Eliminate panic attacks
- Become patient
- Be more productive
- Learn forgiveness
- Ease stress
- Find job satisfaction
- Reduce road rage
- Help with grief
- Reduce aggression
- Increase compassion
- Increase happiness
- Rise above petty issues
- Cure phobias
- Help feel vital
- Have more wisdom
- Quit smoking
- Increase intelligence
- Improve sports performance
- Help with ADD and ADHD
- Increase creativity
- Increase your ability to learn
- Improve your memory
- Help with problem solving
- Reduce eating disorders

- Improve listening skills
- Increase motivation
- Overcome chemical dependencies
- Sharpen your mind
- Increase focus and concentration
- Improve judgement
- Break bad habits
- Increase mental balance
- Develop willpower
- Control your thought patterns
- Increase self-esteem
- Improve self-discipline
- Activate the law of attraction
- Experience enlightenment
- Open your third eye
- Increase intuition
- Find oneness
- Find your purpose
- Expand your consciousness
- Open your heart
- Heal yourself
- Accept yourself and others
- Find peace of mind
- Be one with God
- Experience universal love

More of What Happens When You Meditate

When you meditate your heart rate and respiration slow. Your brain waves slow from the usual thirteen to thirty cycles per second (cps) (which is beta or active outwardly focused level of consciousness) to eight to thirteen cps (the alpha level, a more inwardly focused expanded state of awareness).

The activity in your brain shifts from the right frontal cortex to the left. Richard Davidson, PhD, a researcher at the University of Wisconsin, has been studying meditation's effects on the brain since 2008. He has done a remarkable study on the brains of Buddhist monks to see how meditation affected their neural physiology. He discovered that the part of the brain linked to happiness (left frontal cortex) was more active in the monks then in people who don't meditate.

In meditation, the brain makes more endorphins, the proteins that enhance positive feelings. A study[1] conducted by the Women's Health Initiative on ninety-seven thousand subjects found positive, optimistic people enjoy longer healthier lives than their negative pessimistic peers.

According to a UCLA study[2] led by Eileen Luder, Ph.D., the part of the brain that increases in size when we meditate regularly is the part associated with attention, focus, and positive emotions.

Meditation today is an umbrella for a number of techniques, all leading to an altered state of consciousness (a change in our brain waves).

Beta 12–40hz
Associated with alert and focused concentration, a person in conversation, sports, working, outward mental activities.

---

[1] "Optimism, cynical hostility, and incident coronary heart disease and mortality", by Tindle, H.A., Chang, Y.F., Kuller, L.H. et al. Published 2009;120:656–662, *Women's Health Initiative*, Circulation
[2] "The underlying anatomical correlates of long-term meditation: larger hippocampal and frontal volumes of gray matter", by E Luder, Toga AW, Lepore N, Gaser C. Published 2009, 45(3):672-8, *NeuroImage Journal*

Alpha 8–12hz

Slower frequencies, relaxed mental awareness or inward reflection; a person watching TV or a movie unaware of surroundings slips into alpha. Typically associated with visualization, problem solving, deeper creativity, and contemplation.

Theta 4–8hz

Slower brainwaves and frequencies again, deeper relaxation and meditation, enhanced creativity, light sleep, dreaming, renewal of overall well-being.

Delta 0–4hz

Slowest frequency—deep sleep; it is possible to train yourself to remain awake while reaching the delta state in deeper meditation.

Gamma 40–100hz

The most rapid frequency; seems to link information from all parts of the brain in meditation. They are associated with feelings of blessing or insight. When monks were meditating on compassion, their brains went into gamma. One theory suggests these brain waves contribute to unity of consciousness.

Author Erica Brealy wrote a lovely book called *The Spirit of Meditation*. She gave me permission to include the following excerpts from her book on the explanation of meditation. I highly recommend you purchase this for your library.

Meditation is a state

Meditation is a state you slip into, a bit like when you drift into sleep and, just as sleep can be anything from a light nap to dream-filled deep slumber, so meditation can be experienced in many ways and on many levels, with more or less intensity.

An expansive awareness and spaciousness arise in meditation and a deep inner calm. Timelessness and a consciousness of the 'is-ness" of the moment are also common features.

Meditation is a practice

Meditation is a state of being rather than doing, but paradoxically to experience it you have to try 'doing' it.

A few people – usually advanced meditators – find their minds turn inwards with ease and settle quite naturally into stillness, but the vast majority of us need to employee techniques to help quieten our minds and reach meditation.

Meditation is process

Through regular practice the layers of thought and emotion that block our view of the inner landscape are cleared away and we begin to get glimpses of a different reality. We may have all kinds of meditation experiences – light, visions, intuitions, feelings of love or bliss, an almost tangible sensation of energy flowing through the body, often in the region of the spine, altered patterns of breathing or spontaneous physical movements and momentary flashes of an enlightened state. These are signs of progress, though they can distract and hold us back if we get hooked on them.

Dramatic as they can be, meditation is not just about having a few experiences: it is about inner transformation. Regularly dipping in the still waters of the inner space gradually permeates our everyday lives. We are more able to remain calm and centred and bounce back more quickly from setbacks. On a deeper level we enter into a new relationship with our own consciousness, gradually, uncovering aspects of ourselves that may have been hidden or blocked off[3].

———

Please do not hurry through this book. *Do not even read ahead.* Let each week unfold some new awareness of yourself. Just giving yourself permission to take ten to twenty minutes a day for yourself and actually doing it, can make a quiet shift within you toward the You Who Lives Within.

We have made busyness a kind of god. It seems we think the busier we are, the more we prove our worthiness. We try to find ourselves outside, never filling that emptiness inside. *We are doing it backward.* When we are full of all that we are and know it, our joy becomes enormous. At that moment, there is no need to prove worthiness. We discover that an overabundance of love, creativity, joy, enthusiasm, wonder, curiosity, and passion is who we are. Then all we want is to share all that we are with the world. *We then live and create out of the love of it or the joy of it.*

Another way I could explain it is with the example I give in my spiritual intensive classes. I call it the *great zucchini law of love.* Anyone who has ever grown zucchinis knows they are prolific. After you have made every zucchini recipe you know and frozen even more, you start giving them away. You plead with people, "Take them! Take

---

[3] Erica Brealy, *The Spirit of Meditation.* (Toronto, Ont: McArthur & Co, 2004), pages 26-27

n!" because you know there are many, many more coming. You
e overflowing with zucchinis, and more are coming!

When we realize we are endowed with an endless flow of love and
all her happy companions, then we can joyfully create anything in
the world, always knowing we have more than enough to hold on to
and share with the world. We know more is coming. *We then begin to
create just for the love and joy of creating.*

There are many meditation techniques. As beginners we use them
to help the mind focus. They help us discover and explore the rich
landscape of our inner selves. Eventually you will not need them. You
may even come to long for stillness. It will become natural and easy
for you to spend time within the stillness of you. The time will come
when you are able to live and function in the world while holding to
the quiet center of yourself.

At the end of each chapter, there is space for notes and insights about
your weekly practice. Keep track of your experiences in meditation.
A mediation diary can be very helpful, bringing your inner world to
print and making it a part of your outer experience.

Approach your meditation time as if were a gift—*a gift of you to
yourself.* During your time in meditation you, dear reader, will unwrap
layers and layers of color, emotional thoughts, images, and sensations
that drape your gift. Cherish each layer. Make the unwrapping as
sweet as the gift discovered.

Enjoy your practice time. Shut off the phone, close the doors, and
use a beautiful timer (a soft chime perhaps) to announce the end of

your meditation time. Do each week one day at a time. Repeat the week if you wish.

Master it.

Then move to the next week.

Let's begin.

Sacred Space

Week 1—Making Space for Meditation

Let's start, dear reader, by creating a space for your ten- to twenty-minute meditation. Make it quiet, sacred, and special.

The habit of going to the same place in your home or office space to meditate helps encourage the quieting process—especially when you are new to meditating. Later you will be able to meditate anywhere at any time. The time will come when you live your whole life in an altered, meditative state, quietly heart-centered in a state of love, peace, or appreciation, and greeting each wonder or disaster the same.

To create your space, you need to know what helps create feelings and thoughts of quiet, peace, beauty, harmony, and love *in you*.

Inner Awareness/Outer Awareness

For every outer experience or stimulus, you have an inner response. Most of us are barely aware of our inner responses, yet we make our decisions from that barely conscious state or response.

You choose your coffee cup by how it makes you feel. What you wear, what you eat, the names you call your pets, nicknames you give your loved ones, and the things you buy are all decisions made by how you feel. It all comes from your inner response to them. In our lives we are more outwardly focused. In meditation we strive for an inward focus.

When we become *equally* aware of our inner response to any outer stimulus, we experience "the present." Being in the present, in "the now," or in "the moment" allows us to disconnect from the presumptions of the past or expectations of the future. We often experience a kind of *aha* moment standing in the present. My students speak of experiencing freedom, peace, an undiscovered truth of who they are, or happiness in their present.

When you, dear reader, live like this, you will be able to *choose* your own wonderful response, no matter what outward activity you are participating in.

Exercise 1—First Week: Creating an Awareness and Space for Meditation in Your Life

This exercise will help you to recognize your inner responses to outer stimulation.

1. There is a series of symbols on the following pages. Take your time. Look at each symbol individually, and become aware of your inner response to each one.

   How does it make you feel? How does it affect your mindset? Do you have a physical response to it? If so, what is that?

   Note paper has been provided at the end of this chapter.

2. After you have reviewed the symbols, try this exercise with colors.

3. After colors, try textures; and after textures, try fragrances.

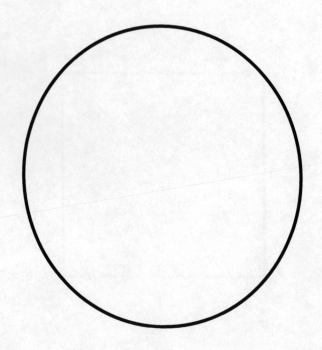

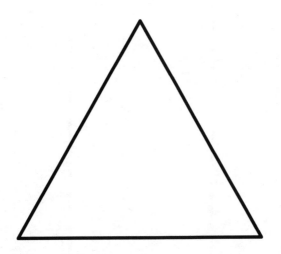

When you are aware of your response, you can use that response to create an environment *just right for you*, lovely reader.

For example, if the straight line "|" created or increased thought, list-making urges, or a feeling of physical restlessness, you would not put pole lights or wallpaper with lines in your bedroom. They may, however, be perfect for the office or family room.

If the horizontal line "—" brought a feeling of peace, then you could put furniture that created a horizontal look or pictures with horizons in your bedroom to encourage peace and rest.

Spend the week going through your coffee cups, dishes, furniture, pictures, candles, books, music, linen closets, shoes, and clothes, and discover what you have surrounded yourself with.

Get rid of everything that elicits a negative inner response. We are letting go of what is not you anymore and making room for new expressions of your true self.

1. Rearrange furniture into a new pattern. See how your family responds.
2. Create a space to meditate in. Even if it is a chair in a corner of the room, make that corner your peace corner.
3. Place in your meditative space objects, pillows, blankets, fragrances, pictures, and books that calm and delight you. Eventually just entering this space moves you to some level of quiet.
4. Have fun with this!

Suggested Reading: Xorin Balkes, *Soul Space*, Novato, Cal., New World Library, ISBN: 978-1-60868-037-5

Insights on Week 1

_____

_____

_____

_____

_____

_____

_____

_____

_____

_____

_____

_____

_____

_____

_____

_____

_____

_____

Breathe

Week 2—Breathing Meditations

Now that we have our special space, we can begin our first step.

Guidelines:

- These exercises must be experienced in order to generate change, not just intellectually understood. Knowing the recipes doesn't change your hunger; cooking and eating does.

- Speaking of eating, avoid meditating within two hours of a heavy meal; you might fall asleep and miss the experience.

- Wear comfortable clothes. If you enjoy sitting cross-legged, in a lotus position, or on a meditation pillow, that is great. Choose a position you can easily hold for twenty minutes. If you are sitting in a chair, make sure your feet can touch the ground without strain. Use a footstool or pillow if needed. If you are lying down, a pillow under the knees can be helpful for the lower back, and a small pillow under the head. Mats are readily available in yoga and camping centers. Some people like to sit on cushions with their back against the wall for support, or they prefer to place cushions against the wall for more support.

- Use blankets and pillows to keep you warm and comfortable.

- Now we are free to focus inward.

ⓢ Soft, meditative music is also helpful. I will recommend some with each exercise.

ⓢ Maintain a passive attitude (by that I mean a lack of concern about how well you are doing; it means uncritically feeling yourself in the present).

ⓢ No expectations (they can limit the meditative experience).

ⓢ Meditate every day. It does not matter if you do it morning, noon, or night. Whenever you can meditate is the perfect time for you. Some people find doing it the same time every day helps to make it part of their daily routine.

ⓢ If your mind wanders—which it will—smile. Acknowledge it and then turn back to your focus. If your body gets sore or restless—which it will—smile, acknowledge it, and turn back to your focus. If emotions come up, whether they are lovely or scary—which they will—smile, acknowledge it, and turn back to your focus.

As you practice meditation, you will come to recognize you are not your body. You are not your mind. You are not your emotions. You are something *more* …

Why Do We Use Smiling in Our Meditation Exercises?

Besides making you even more beautiful or handsome, dear reader, smiling also does the following:

ⓢ changes your mood (as studies have shown that smiling releases endorphins, natural pain killers, and serotonin)
ⓢ reduces your blood pressure
ⓢ boosts your immune system

ⓥ relieves stress

ⓥ keeps you positive

My students have noticed that when asked to smile at nothing in particular (try it now), their hearts warm and they relax and find it easy to let go. In this lovely state, the heart and mind link and give you a new way of experiencing your life—even thinking becomes less critical and more creative. Try it again now.

Try it throughout your day. Notice the inward change with this outward action. You may discover with a smile that your outer situations appear a little different. You may also find solutions you hadn't previously thought of coming to your mind. Use your note paper at the end of the chapter to write out your experiences.

Breathing

♩ ♪ '   Suggested Music: *"Angel Love"* by Aeoliah

All of our meditations start with some kind of breathing technique or focus. I have included a few for you to practice this week. Each of these techniques can be a meditation practice on their own.

Breathing Meditation I

1. Set your timer for ten minutes.

2. Sit for this exercise.

3. Close your eyes.

4. This is very simple—just observe yourself breathing.

5. Notice the air coming into your nose and then notice it leaving through your nose or mouth. Notice the sensation of air coming into your lungs, and notice the sensation of air leaving your lungs.

6. Do nothing else.

7. If your mind wanders—smile, acknowledge it, and turn back to breathing.

Yeah! You have just meditated!

Questions to ask yourself after the meditation:

- What is my state of mind?
- What is my state of emotion?
- What is my state of body?
- What is different after this meditation?

Breathing Meditation 2

It sounds more complicated than it is experienced. Read through the instructions, and then read through while you practice the breathing. Once you have it, practice for ten minutes.

In this meditation "____" means pause.

1. Set your timer for ten minutes.

2. You may sit or lie down for this exercise.

3. Close your eyes.

4. Inhale through your nose; exhale with a soft whooshing sound through your mouth.

5. Take long, slow inhales and long, slow exhales.

6. As you inhale, fill your abdomen, your diaphragm, and your chest. Notice the ribs expanding.

7. Hold your breath ____ smile ____.

8. Exhale slowly ____. Pull your abdomen in, releasing all of the air.

9. Hold empty for a moment ____ smile ____.

10. Begin again.

After the meditation, do an inward check and make notes:

- What is the state of my body?
- What is the state of my emotions?
- What is the state of my mind?
- What is the difference in me since the meditation?

Breathing Meditation 3

This meditation is a ten- to fifteen-minute meditation—whichever you are comfortable with.

Breathing with a count can be very helpful for busy minds or when you find yourself distressed by something. The counting helps focus the mind, pulling it away from what's wrong and instead placing it into you in the present. Remember "____" means pause.

1. Set your timer.

2. Repeat Breathing Meditation 2. However, this time add a count to the inhale. ____ hold ____ exhale ____ hold ____.

3. Perhaps you may find as you start your meditation that you can inhale to the count of four and hold for the count of two. Exhale to the count of four and hold empty for two.

4. As you relax and get comfortable with this technique, it will lengthen perhaps to a count of six and hold of three.

5. Feel free to practice these breathing techniques with your eyes open while driving, walking, shopping, working, gardening, and just living.

Some studies[4] have reported the discovery of a direct relationship between brain activity and the nasal cycle and with alternations of congestion and decongestion in the nasal passages (about forty-five-minute cycles). When airflow moves more freely in one nostril, the opposite hemisphere of the brain is relatively more dominant.

Forceful breathing through the more congested nostril awakens the less-dominant hemisphere. EEG responses showed a consistent relationship between nasal airflow and cerebral dominance in all frequencies (alpha, theta, delta, beta).

---

[4] "Selective hemispheric stimulation by unilateral forced nostril breathing", by DA Werntz, RG Bickford, D Shannahoff-Khalsa. Published 1987, 6(3):165-71, *Human Neurobiology* ; "The ultradian rhythm of alternating cerebral hemispheric activity", by D Shannahoff-Khalsa. Published June 1993, 70(3-4):285-98, *International Journal of Neuroscience*

Remember the study of Buddhist monks, published in the *New York Times* in 2003,[5] used magnetic resonance imagining (MRI) to view the effects of meditation on their brains. The brain scans showed that as a result of meditation, the left prefrontal cortex (the site of joy) predominated over the right prefrontal cortex (the site on anxiety) in the monks.

Becoming Aware of Nasal Dominance

Do this exercise on and off *throughout the day*, finding the timing of your cyclic rhythm.

1. Check inwardly for your state of being.

2. Check nostrils to find when you breathe out of both nostrils whether there a regular time to that cycle.

   ℘ Less congestion in left nostril suggests right-brain activities. At these times you will be in a dreamier, more intuitive, creative, and imaginative state. The right brain controls the left side of your body.

   ℘ Less congestion in the right nostril suggests left-brain activity. At these times you will be typically more alert— more prone to practical rational thinking, problem solving, and talking. The left brain controls the right side of your body.

---

[5] "Is Buddhism Good for Your Health?" by Stephen S. Hall. Published September 14, 2003, *New York Times*

Breathing Meditation 4—Alternate Breath

When you first begin doing this meditation exercise, you may feel like you are out of breath or cannot get enough air. That passes as you relax with the breathing technique.

This is a great breathing exercise once you are comfortable with it. It can be used as a manual override. For example, if you can't sleep or wake up in the middle of the night with your brain determined to rewrite or reenact your entire past or make lists for tomorrow or solve all the world's problems, you know, dear reader, that you are breathing in through the right nostril, activating the left brain, and it's ready for action.

Doing this exercise can get you breathing from the right nostril, calming and relaxing the mind. And soon you will be sleeping.

Another example is if you are at work and your brain wants to sleep or is sluggish. Doing this exercise and switching to inhaling from the right nostril can wake up the left side of the brain and get you productive again. It is also great when you have a cold. Sit in the tub with a hot cloth over your nose, inhaling the heat and steam. Have plenty of tissues ready.

This does call for a little hand-eye coordination so you will want to practice first. Use your thumb and ring finger of the same hand to open and close nostrils. Your index and middle fingers rest softly between your eyebrows. Practice a few times just moving your thumb and ring finger to open and close the nostrils. When you are ready, begin.

If you are doing this in the morning, end the exercise by breathing in through your right nostril, so you will be ready for the day. If you are doing this at night, finish the exercise by breathing in through the left nostril. This will help you to wind down for sleep.

Do this meditation sitting. Read first, then read again and practice the exercise until you are comfortable with the actions.

Practice the second breathing technique while doing the alternate breath.

1. Use right thumb to close off right nostril. Inhale slowly through the left nostril, expanding your belly, your diaphragm, and your chest.

2. Close off both nostrils and hold full.

3. Open your left nostril by lifting your ring finger and exhale slowly out the left nostril.

4. Close off both nostrils and hold empty.

5. Repeat for ten times.

6. Breathe normally and do an inward check.

7. Now repeat the exercise, inhaling through the right nostril, exhaling through the left.

This is one round. Do one or two rounds per meditation period.

Good luck this week. Give yourself permission to enjoy these exercises. Take your time and savor the quiet that is you.

Notes and Insights on Week 2

Relax

Week 3—Relaxation Meditations

𝄞 ♪ ˀ Suggested Music: *Any of the Reiki Massage music is good for this week's practice.*

All of our meditations from this point on begin with some form of breathing and relaxation. Dear reader, you cannot have the feeling of warm well-being in your body and at the same time experience psychological stress.

Deep relaxation when successfully mastered can and has been used as a way of reducing your blood pressure and heart rate. It has been used to stop your fight-or-flight response, stop anxiety, reduce pain, and increase your body's natural healing response.

Progressive Relaxation

Sometimes we are so busy in our lives and our heads that we are unaware of the tension we carry or seem unable to let go of the projects, plans, work, expectations, guilt, and pain. This exercise is very good for releasing those tensions.

It can be done sitting, but most of my students find lying down for this the best. If you are lying down, support your head and use a blanket. Sometimes a pillow under the knees can help the back.

Read the instructions, then read and do the exercise. When you have the process memorized, as Nike says, "Just do it!"

Enjoy this one ♡.

Rest in the relaxation as long as your time permits. Because we are beginners just starting out, aim for fifteen minutes, gradually lengthening that time. Setting a gentle timer eliminates the concern about, "Is it time?"

When you are at your deepest place of relaxation, do an inward check and name the emotion you feel.

Relaxation 1—Progressive Relaxation

Here again in this meditation, "____" means pause. Pause for ten seconds.

1. Start with three to five minutes of Breathing Meditation 2

2. Tighten the muscles of your forehead by raising your eyebrows; notice the tension ____. Then let it go; let it relax and become smooth. ____

3. Now smile extra wide; notice the tension ____. Let it go; relax and soften the face. ____

4. Gently look up at the ceiling ____; bring your head forward, chin to chest. Notice the tension ____. Bring your head back to resting, letting the tension go, relaxing the neck, shoulders, and back of head. ____

5. Now clench your fist; notice the tension ____. Let it go, and let the arms and hands relax. ____

6. Flex you biceps; notice the tension ____. Let them relax. Again let the arms, the forearms, and the hands relax. ____

7. Shrug your shoulders; notice the tension ____. Now push the shoulders down and notice the tension ____. Let it go; relax. Take a deep breath and relax again on the exhale. ____

8. Take a deep breath and push out your stomach like a balloon; notice the tension ____. Exhale and relax. ____

9. Tighten your buttocks notice the tension ____. Let them go; let them relax.____

10. Flex your toes; pull them toward the knees. Notice the tension ____. Now curl your toes and notice the tension ____. Let the toes go and relax. ____

11. Feel a warmth spread through your body starting at your feet and moving up through the top of your head. Rest in this warmth and relaxation for ten to fifteen minutes.

The feeling and words you discover at your deepest relaxation point can be used as your special doorway to relaxation. This relaxation technique will help you and your body remember what relaxation feels like. Check through the day for any tension your body expresses. Then quickly exaggerate it and release as easily as a breath in and a breath out.

Relaxation 2—Relax and Breathe Meditation

Read through the instructions first. Read and follow it. Then, dear reader, r-eee-llll-aaxx. *In this meditation, rest for twenty seconds or so when prompted.* If you like fragrance, seek out pure essential oils that encourage relaxation for you.

1. Start with five minutes of Breathing Meditation 2.

2. Inhale, feeling and visualizing the breath going into your feet and ankles; hold your breath and admire. Smile. Exhale and relax the feet.

    Rest.

3. Inhale, feeling and visualizing the breath going into your calves and knees; hold your breath and admire. Smile. Exhale and relax the calves and knees.

    Rest.

4. Inhale, feeling and visualizing the breath going into your thighs and buttocks; hold your breath and admire. Smile. Exhale and relax the thighs and buttocks.

    Rest.

5. Inhale, feeling and visualizing the breath going into your abdomen and lower back; hold your breath and admire. Smile. Exhale and relax the abdomen and lower back.

    Rest.

6. Inhale, feeling and visualizing the breath going into your solar plexus and middle back; hold your breath and admire. Smile. Exhale and relax the solar plexus and middle back.

    Rest.

7. Inhale, feeling and visualizing the breath going into your chest and upper back; hold your breath and admire. Smile. Exhale and relax the chest and upper back.

Rest.

8. Inhale, feeling and visualizing the breath going into your shoulders, arms and hands; hold your breath and admire. Smile. Exhale and relax the shoulders, arms and hands.

Rest.

9. Inhale, feeling and visualizing the breath going into your neck; hold your breath and admire. Smile. Exhale and relax the neck.

Rest.

10. Inhale, feeling and visualizing the breath going into your head and face; hold your breath and admire. Smile. Exhale and relax the head and face.

11. Take a deep breath. Sigh.

Rest.

Try a massage this week to help your body enjoy even more relaxation!

Relaxation 3—Inward Body Scan Meditation

This is very different from the first two relaxation techniques. As you approach this meditation, completely let go of your tendency to want things to be different from how they are. *Allow them to be exactly as they are. Don't even try to relax.* Relaxation may happen or it may not. We choose to be inwardly focused and aware of our experiences.

Read and follow the instructions. Then repeat on your own.

1. Begin by feeling the weight of your body on the mat, chair, or bed.

2. Become aware of the sensations of your breath. Really focus on the air passing through your nostrils on the rise and fall of the chest. Observe for up to five minutes.

3. With the same inward focus and with gentle awareness, start at your toes and move through every part of your body. Take your time. Do not hurry. Enjoy this process.

4. Once your body scan is complete, rest. Rest in the comfort of your body, your mind and your emotions at peace.

Know you are complete just as you are. ♡

———

Relaxation 4—Quick Relaxer

Read and follow the instructions. Then repeat on your own. In this meditation, "___" has been extended. Pause for ten to thirty seconds between steps.

1. Start with five minutes of a breathing technique from week two.

2. Bring all your awareness to your feet and tell your feet to relax.

3. Systematically move your awareness through your body, relaxing each and pausing after each for ten to thirty seconds.

    i.   Relax your calves and ankles. ____
    ii. Relax your thighs and knees.____
    iii. Relax your hips and buttocks. ____
    iv. Relax your lower back and belly. ____
    v.   Relax your solar plexus and middle of your back. ____
    vi. Relax your chest and upper back. ____
    vii. Relax your shoulders. ____
    viii. Relax your neck. ____
    ix. Relax both arms and hands. ____
    x.   Relax the back you your head the top of your head. ____
    xi. Relax your head and face. ____

4. Take a deep breath and allow the relaxation to deepen.

Suggested reading: *The Relaxation Response* and *Beyond the Relaxation Response*, by H. Benson

Notes and Insights on Week 3

Mantras

Week 4—Mantra Meditations

♪ ♩ ⸯ   Suggested music CD: *Angel Reiki* by Patrick Bernard

Lovely reader, welcome back! This week's theme is mantras. Mantra in Sanskrit means "man," to think, and "tra," to liberate. Mantras can be a syllable, a word, a name, or even an image that is repeated many times.

Choosing one that has a special meaning to you seems to generate the greatest interest for your mind and heart, making it easier to hold your focus. From the Eastern traditions we have words like *om*, called the great mantra; *so-hum*, I am he; and *sa-hum*, I am she.

Some people use affirmations as a mantra. We, as beginners, will focus on a single word that has meaning to you. We will choose a different word for each day of this week. Some words to consider are: peace, love, calm, joy, relax, health, quiet, harmony, happiness, and stillness. If you enjoy this, there are many small decks available with cards to pull for each day (e.g., the Angel Deck, Be the Change Deck, Virtue Cards). You can use them to select your mantra and focus for the day.

In our first mantra meditation, use your word from week 3's Progressive Relaxation. This style of meditation works very well for busy minds and busy days or days when you are once again trying to rewrite the past.

Repeating the mantra helps you, dear reader, to disconnect from the endless chatter and give you a glimpse into the space between your thoughts. Later the spaces expand and you will begin to experience the quiet that is you, eventually experiencing oneness with all life.

If you are asking, "What space?" think of the last time someone interrupted you and asked you to look at something or a moment when you were surprised or frightened. In that moment your mind suspended thought to focus on something unexpected. It is possible to expand these moments of non-thought or moments of space.

The *attitude* we have as we approach this meditation introduces us to our first meditation dilemma. Our hearts and heads learn differently. We will strive to address both in this meditation.

From the mind's perspective, we are focusing on a word and letting ourselves go deeper into the meaning of that word. It is our single focus. We hang onto it like we would a buoy in the ocean. Whenever your thoughts wander in that ocean of thought, just bring them back to your word and your focus.

From the heart's perspective, we are calling forth the emotion from the center of our eternal self, striving to drink it in and fill ourselves with it. To become it. To know it.

With the mind we go deeper. With the heart, it rises up and fills your whole being; eventually they stop being separate. You become one with all that you are.

Mantra Meditation 1

Read and follow the instructions. Then repeat on your own.

This meditation is best done in a seated position. However, if you wish to lie down, get comfy.

1. Start with five to ten minutes of your favorite breathing exercise.

2. Use your relaxation word from week three.

3. Inhale and on the exhale, say the mantra, extending the word for the length of the exhale. Repeat for two to five minutes.

4. Now repeat step two but shift to whispering your word/ mantra on the exhale. Repeat for two to five minutes.

5. This time on the exhale silently repeat the mantra to yourself.

6. Continue with step five for the length of your meditation time.

When your mind wanders, just smile, acknowledge it and gently bring your mind back to your mantra.

Mantra Meditation 2—Fifteen to Twenty Minutes

1. Start with five to ten minutes of Breathing Exercise 2.

2. Inhale, and fill your heart with the emotion or the feeling of your mantra. Hold it. On the exhale, say the mantra, extending the word for the length of the exhale. Repeat for two to five minutes.

3. Repeat step two, but now shift to whispering your word— your mantra on the exhale. Repeat for two to five minutes.

4. This time on the exhale silently repeat the mantra to yourself.

5. Continue with step four for the length of your meditation time.

Keep your focus equally on the feeling and the thought. Let go and become the mantra.

───────

Mantra Meditation 3, Candle Meditation—Ten to Fifteen Minutes

In this meditation we use the flame of a candle as our focus. The flame acts as a visual mantra for us. Perhaps the most well-known visual mantras are the Buddhist mandalas. If you find they interest you, search out a mandala coloring book and feel yourself slip into a happy altered state as you color.

As you focus on the light of the flame, you may feel pressure on the third eye, the middle of your forehead. This type of meditation can help to develop inner vision. The candle meditation is especially good for quieting the body and the mind. It tends to balance the right and left brain, getting rid of busy chatter, and helps to revive a tired mind. With practice you will get so you can close your eyes and recall the flame anytime.

The thought we carry into this meditation, as we focus on the flame of the candle, is, *We are calling forth the light within.*

1. Sit comfortably with a burning candle in a stand on a table or the floor in front of you.

2. Do three to five minutes of a breathing technique you prefer. *Don't blow out the candle!*

3. With eyes open, focus on the flame. Once you have the image, close your eyes and hold the flame image as long as you can.

   The flame may change to black or red; it may get smaller or move around. Don't let this distract you. When the image disappears, open your eyes and focus on the flame again.

4. Repeat for the duration of your meditation.

You may see colors around the flame at times. Enjoy them. They are the colors of your aura wrapped around the flame. Don't get distracted by them though. Keep your focus on the flame.

Enjoy the quiet. ♡

Feel free to use your mantras as a focus throughout the day. When you are driving, in a line up, or walking, do some deep breathing and use your daily mantra. You may find, dear reader, your day becomes far more enjoyable and you enjoy being you far more. ♡

Have a candle at work, and when you are over-stressed and can't focus, light the candle and center yourself.

Mantra Meditation 4, Om—Ten to Twenty Minutes

Suggested music: There are many CDs with a continuous chant of om. Purchase one and play it in the background. It will add a resonance to your meditation.

1. Repeat Mantra Meditation 1 using om.

2. As you relax, the exhale lengthens and your voice gets stronger. Sing along!

3. Enjoy it. Find the tone that makes your whole body vibrate. And enjoy.

4. Now repeat the mantra. This time go silent. Take the mantra inward.

Have a great week!

Notes and Insights on Week 4

Vision

Week 5—Visualization

Dear reader, we are at week five! How wonderful! Hopefully you have come to cherish your meditation time. Have you noticed changes in you? Have you had glimpses or perhaps moments experiencing the sweetness of your inner self?

This week we venture into the astounding world of visualization. Your mind is miraculous! It does not know the difference between real or imagined experiences. It will change the body and emotions to fit the situation (real or imagined).

The power of your imagination far exceeds that of your will. It is hard to will yourself into a relaxed state but you can imagine yourself on a beach happy, safe, and warm in the sun, hearing birds, listening to the waves, sounds of children laughing, and … relaxation happens.

You know when you think sad thoughts you feel unhappy. If you think anxious thoughts, you become tense. All your thoughts become a reality. Essentially you are who *you think* you are. To overcome the feeling of unhappiness or tension, you, dear reader, can refocus your mind on positive, healing images. Remarkable healings (miracles) have been recorded in the past thirty years as science and meta-science begin to merge.

Visualization is now being recommended to help heal cancer; reduce pain; increase self-esteem; increase sales; improve athletic performance; reduce stress; help in goal achievement, and assist in our path to enlightenment.

Sound too good to be true? It requires one thing: regular, consistent practice!

Visualization Meditation 1—Half Hour or More

This is fun and works well when your head is too busy or too tired to focus. It helps to stimulate your imagination and visualization skills.

♪   Suggested music: Pick three different types of music. Each should be piece approximately ten minutes. Choose music without words: classical-romantic, meditation, and healing music.

Use headphones or ear buds or turn the music up loud.

1. Lie down. Breathe and let the music play through you.

2. Give your mind permission to envision colors, light movement, images, and symbols that go with your music.

Music and mind playing together.

≈

Visualization Meditation 2—I Am the Flame—Ten to Thirty Minutes

Suggested music: "Reiki" by Merlin's Magic

This is an extension of our Candle Meditation. Dear reader, you can do five to ten minutes of the candle meditation first and then move on to this one. Your choice. ♡

Read through the instructions until you have it and then begin.

1. Sit comfortably.

2. Begin with the Breathing Meditation 2 for five minutes.

3. Breathe normally. Gently rest your awareness on your heart for approximately three minutes.

4. Become aware of a small flame within the center of your heart. With each inhale, the flame grows until your entire body is aglow in a pure, golden/white light.

5. Rest in the warmth and love for five to ten minutes.

6. Visualize this warm, loving, spiritual light radiating out beyond you, touching everyone and everything in your life.

7. In the same way a candle lights and warms a room, warm the spaces of your life—the open spaces and the dark spaces—until light and warmth and love are all there is in your life. Now rest.

Visualization Meditation 3, the Meadow—Thirty Minutes or More

Read through the instructions first … and maybe a second time! Then begin.

1. Lay or sit comfortably.

2. Start with a favorite breathing exercise.

3. Continue with a relaxation meditation from week 3.

4. Visualize and feel yourself walking down a sunlit path with huge trees on each side. Include as many senses as possible: What does it smell like? What do you see? Hear? How does it feel to walk with the sun on your shoulders, etc.?

5. Notice the feeling of freedom and peace growing in you as you walk. The path leads to an open meadow. Visualize anything you want in this meadow: a stream, a pond, trees, flowers, fragrance, sounds. Create the perfect place to regenerate yourself.

6. As you lay on the grass or a favorite rock looking up at the sky, feel blessed. Give thanks for all the good in your life.

7. Rest in that feeling of being blessed.

≈

Visualization Meditation 4, Relax and Let Go— Twenty to Thirty Minutes

This lovely meditation can be done on its own or as a prelude to a healing meditation. We are visualizing and feeling memories, hurts, and guilt leaving our body. It's not hard. It only takes focus and your willingness, dear reader, to be done with it.

Read through the instructions a couple of times until you have it down. Enjoy the release!

The attitude we take into this meditation is one of great tenderness and kindness.

1. Start by lying down. Get very comfy!

2. Do ten minutes of your favorite breathing exercise.

3. If you have a problem area, start there. Work through your body and then return to the problem area and do it again. Otherwise begin at your hands and work through your entire body.

4. Feel and visualize your hands for ten to thirty seconds.

5. Tell them to relax and let go. Visualize all the times you reached for someone and he or she was not there. Recall the times you hammered your finger, stuck a needle into your finger, or broke your hand. All those wounded memories. Feel and visualize them leaving as a ghost-like copy of your hands, disappearing like a mist into the universe. You may feel sensations as they leave. When they have left, feel your hands elongate or stretch and relax.

6. Smile.

7. Whisper to your hands, "Thank you."

8. Move through your entire body this way.

9. When you have finished, *rest* and enjoy the deep relaxation and peace in your body.

This next meditation can be done right after the fourth (Relax and Let Go), if you have time.

Visualization Meditation 5, Self-Healing—Thirty and Sixty Minutes

Dear Reader, there are many, many techniques for self-healing. This is a simple yet profound meditation. Take your time. *Fall in love with yourself.*

Do this meditation lying down.

1. Start with a favorite breathing exercise.

2. If you have not done the Relax and Let Go beforehand, choose the quick relaxer from week 3.

3. Resting in your heart, bring up the feeling of love. If you can't find the feeling, think of a time when your heart warmed to love (e.g., a puppy, a baby, a kitten, a sunset, a loved one).

4. Send that love to your toes and silently whisper to them, "I love you." Fill your toes with so much love they release whatever is "not love" in order to hold the love. Let them relax into that love.

5. Slowly repeat this process throughout your entire body.

6. When you have done the whole body, visualize yourself surrounded and floating in a golden/white cocoon of love.

7. Rest here. Let your body and heart rest in the delight and healing of love.

Visualization Meditation 6, Forgiveness—Ten to Thirty Minutes

What we don't forgive, we are destined to live or live in constant attack and defense, expecting it to happen again. It puts barriers between us and everyone else in our lives, not just the individual involved or our selves.

When we choose to forgive (and it is a choice!), we are saying to ourselves, "I no longer wish to be defined by this wound and stay frozen here. I choose to learn and grow from this." Freedom!

This can be done lying down or sitting.

Make yourself *very* comfortable. Sometimes the profound and courageous act of forgiving can bring up body sensations. Being warm helps to let them go rather than tensing up and holding on to them.

Dearest reader, the attitude you hold as you approach this mediation is one of kindness to yourself and pride in yourself that you are willing and ready to become more than you have ever been. Forgiveness releases the ties to your past. You are then free to live a new adventure.

Read the instructions through and then begin.

1. Start with a breathing exercise for five minutes.

2. Follow with a deep relaxation from week three.

3. Visualize or feel the person's presence before you. If this is about you forgiving you, visualize yourself in front of you.

4. Allow yourself to experience all the feelings you have toward this person, place, or thing. Say to the person, place, or thing the following:

   + "I am now ready to forgive and let this go." Rest for thirty to sixty seconds.

   + "I thank you for teaching me *(whatever you have learned)*." Rest. Smile. Rest for thirty to sixty seconds.

   + "I forgive you. May you be happy."

5. Let the person go.

You may have to do this more than once. When you stop feeling resistance to the choice of forgiveness and feel a neutral feeling or a warm, gentle glow in your heart, you have it! Dear reader, you are free to remember without pain. You are free to create a future and a present without the influence of that situation or past hurt. You can begin to create from your own goodness.

Congrats!

Notes and Insights on Week 5

The early benefits of meditation are often felt in the physical body and emotions, increasing relaxation and your general sense of well-being. It brings clarity and better focus, even calmness to the mind.

Meditation not only balances the body but can also give us access to the many subtle worlds that surround us. When that happens, it changes our view of reality forever. You may see, hear, or feel color. You may see, hear, or feel sound. Visions of the past, present, or future may appear. Sometimes you may experience loved ones who have passed over, sharing a message. Angels, fairies, animals, or lights may appear or speak to you. Symbols may fade into your vision or knowing and then fade out. Some people hear the most beautiful music. You may sense people standing or floating around you, guiding or encouraging you. Sometimes you come out of meditation with answers to questions or a problem you have been working over. Other times you are inspired toward something totally new for you.

Some people experience swaying, rocking, changes in breathing, and feelings of heat or coolness. Some feel tingling or energy moving through their bodies. Some people are filled with great joy; others cry because their hearts are overwhelmed with love. Meditation can cause emotional and mental clearings. As you fill yourself with new light-filled and loved-filled experiences, old toxic emotions or thoughts rise to the surface to be released. It can be quite surprising. All of these experiences are gifts. Learn. Observe. Love. Thank each experience and release it.

Once you have been meditating for some time, your meditations may seem too familiar, stale, even boring. Then you will question if meditation works for you—or worse yet, you may think you are failing at it. You might want to back away. *Do not! Stay with it.* It is a sign you are outgrowing yourself. Yeah! Try changing your routine around a little. Keep meditating. Even boredom is a sign of progress.

Affirmations

Week 6—Self-Hypnosis and Affirmations

Suggested music: "Shamanic Dream" by Anugama

You are no stranger to hypnosis. Anytime you daydream or tell someone about a book you read or a movie you've watched, you slip into a type of self-induced hypnosis as you remember and recall. When driving long distances or watching TV, you tend to "lose yourself" in concentration. This too is a type of self-hypnosis.

Self-hypnosis is a wonderful form of meditation for healing the body, the mind, and the emotions. With it, we can access the subconscious and reprogram ourselves. And this is where affirmations come in.

To affirm something by definition means to declare something to be true. When we use self-hypnosis to access the subconscious, we can place an affirmation and its accompanying visualization directly into our subconscious, telling ourselves we are choosing this as our new truth. It helps to repeat the affirmation throughout the day, at the same time bringing up the visualization and feelings associated with it.

It's the subconscious's job to make your predominant thoughts or goals real in your life. It will organize the entire universe to make you right. To your subconscious, whatever you are obsessing about is your goal. Since most of us obsess about what's wrong or the past, we keep repeating the same things over and over.

Affirmations give us something positive to create in our lives. Yes!

Week 6, Affirmation Meditation—Twenty to Forty Minutes

The affirmation we will use was first used in the 1800s. *It has that kind of staying power.* We are using it daily throughout the week.

> "Every day in every way, I am getting better and better."

Do this lying down or sitting. Most of my students prefer to lie down for this one.

Read through first and then begin with an attitude of quiet joy.

1. Start with a ten-minute breathing exercise.

2. Do a favorite relaxation.

3. Visualize yourself on a set of stairs. Each step is lit and numbered.

   ☺ As you walk down the stairs, feel yourself moving down. Watch the number of each step as you go, starting at thirty.

   ☺ At the bottom of the stairs, there is a hallway leading to many rooms. You are looking for the computer room. The name is on the door.

   ☺ Go to the door. Open it and turn on the light.

   ☺ There is a large screen and in front of it, a chair and a keyboard. Sit in the chair.

   At the keyboard, type in your affirmation: "Every day in every way, I am getting better and better."

- As you visualize, notice it appearing on the screen in front of you.

- Sit back and visualize all the ways you are getting better and better. Use as many senses as you can.

- Enrich the visualization with all your senses.

- Spend as much time here as you like.

  When you are ready to leave the computer room, type the following at the keyboard: "I want this repeated seven hundred thousand times."

- Get up out of the chair, leave the light on, and leave the room. Walk down the hallway to the stairs. Because we don't need to return to the same level of tension we started with, there are only ten steps to. Take the stairs up.

- Before opening your eyes, do an internal check. Notice how you feel. Smile. And greet your new life!

There are many websites and books listing affirmations. Do a bit of research and find some that fit you. As a beginner only work on one affirmation at a time. Use it for two weeks. Let it go for two weeks and then pick it up again. Repeat this until you see or feel it in action in your life.

Look for an older book: Joseph Murphy Ph. D., D.D., *The Power of the Subconscious Mind*, Penguin Publication Group, ISBN: 978-0-73520-431-7. It is worth the hunt.

Notes and Insights on Week 6

Love

Week 7—Love

𝄞 ♪ ᵇ   Suggested music: "Reiki Healing" by Deuter

We are so used to being the mind. It can take a number of tries before we get the concept of watching our thoughts. Practice it during the day. A few seconds here, a minute there. It can be a huge *aha* moment when you "know" you are not your thoughts. Then it dawns on you—you are also not your emotions or your body.

You are the one watching! Who is that watcher? That, dear reader, is the beginning of your spiritual quest—to re-remember:

You are God's child, a divine being. You are love incarnate, cleverly disguised as a mere human! ♡

Week 7, Meditation I, Being Present—Twenty to Forty Minutes

Read the instructions, then get comfortable; sit or lie down for this meditation.

There are no bad thoughts and no good thoughts—just thoughts. The mind repeats thoughts. Some say 95 percent of our thoughts are about the past and we create scenarios with these thoughts. That does not make the thoughts true. You do not have to act or react to every thought.

The attitude we carry into the meditation is curiosity, acceptance, and compassion.

1. Become aware of your breathing—the sound, the chest's movement, the air moving in and out of your nostrils. Do this for five minutes.

2. Do the Body Scan exercise from week three.

3. Now turn your attention to your inner thoughts. Just be present with them. Watch. Listen. Have no judgment or criticism—just open acceptance and compassion. Do this for ten minutes.

4. Smile. Can you create a distance or space between your thoughts? Can you focus on the space in the same manner as you do a thought? Can you observe yourself observing?

Take as much time on this as you wish.

Give yourself the delicious luxury of being present with you here and throughout your day. ♡

Some—myself included—believe that everything in our world is conscious: people, water, fire, plants, animals, soil, crystals, cells, bacteria, viruses, the earth, the planets, and the stars. We are woven together like a great piece of lace or a web or a matrix of *love*. This love is intelligent.

Miraculously, the cells and the DNA of your body are each individually conscious and woven together in *love* for *the you who lives within*.

This you is sacred, loving, joyful, all powerful, peaceful, and magic. Your body knows this you to be the God within.

If you sit quietly, coming to yourself without needs or wants and holding a loving curiosity, this you envelops everything you are and you begin to remember who *you are*.

Week 7, Meditation 2, You Who Lives Within— Twenty to Forty Minutes

Read through and enjoy the ♡ doing ♡. Again here, the "____" represents a thirty- to sixty-second pause.

1. Sit for this meditation.

2. Fix your eyes on a spot on the floor before you. ____

3. Become aware of your breath. Notice the air moving in and out. Notice the feeling of the air passing through nostrils, into your lungs, and then leaving again. Do this for five minutes.

4. Allow yourself to appreciate the deepening relaxation and calmness. ____

5. Now let your eyes close.

6. Appreciate the change in you as your awareness moves deeper inside yourself.

7. Notice with every exhale your relaxation deepens for five minutes. Enjoy.

8. Sit quietly breathing.

9. Bring up the feeling of love in your heart. If you find it difficult, think of someone you love or a special time when you were loving or a basket of puppies!

10. Send love through your heart to the You Who Lives Within.

11. Continuing to send love, just listen; feel, appreciate, and receive. ____

12. If your mind wanders, bring it back to the breath and sending love to the You Who Lives Within.

Week 7, Meditation 3—Finding Consciousness

For this meditation you will need a rock or a crystal, a plant, and running water, like a fountain or a stream.

Read through. Enjoy!

1. This can be done inside or out.

2. Sit focusing on or holding the rock or crystal.

3. Do your favorite breathing exercise.

4. Keep your eyes focused on your object. Send love or appreciation through your heart to the object.

5. Relax into the object for ten minutes.

6. Can you recognize the living consciousness of the object?

7. Now switch to the plant and repeat.

8. Can you recognize the living consciousness of the plant?

For the water meditation, follow the above instructions and:

1. Relax into the water for thirty seconds to one minute.

2. Relax into the sound of the water for thirty seconds to one minute.

3. Love the sound as much as the water for ten minutes.

4. Can you find the living consciousness of the water?

Notes and Insights on Week 7

It is time to start at the beginning of the book again. As you rediscover inner and outer awareness, refer to your notes.

   ⊚ Make new notes; take time to enjoy the changes in you.

   ⊚ Do recreate your meditation space.

   ⊚ Use your breathing techniques as complete meditations, spending fifteen to thirty minutes just breathing.

   ⊚ Notice the changes, and celebrate each progression.

Lovely reader, hopefully our short, shared time together has awakened a new connection with the truth of you. This is just the beginning of your meditation journey. If you continue I can promise your world will become profoundly enriched.

It is a gentle journey. Don't hurry. Don't compare. Have fun and take the time to appreciate the wonder of who you are.

Printed in the United States
By Bookmasters

CPSIA information can be obtained at www.ICGtesting.com
Printed in the USA
LVOW121628020412

275807LV00011B/37/P